Governmental Accounting 101: Accounts Payable Best Practices

SADANAND PUJARI

Published by SADANAND PUJARI, 2023.

Table of Contents

Copyright

Governmental Accounting 101: Accounts Payable Best Practices

First Edition: Dec 2023

Book Design by **SADANAND PUJARI**

About

Governmental accounting, including fund accounting financial transactions, focusing on the general fund and government-wide activities.

We will work through many example problems as we learn the material, posting transactions to a trial balance, so we can see how accounts behave. Many governmental accounts are new to many learners, and we will be using different accounting methods than just an accrual method. Posting transactions and seeing a trial balance will be very helpful in learning the material and is something lacking in most Books on the subject.

We will discuss the governmental accounting objectives and reporting requirements, comparing them to for-profit entities. The Book will assume we are familiar with for-profit accounting and will, therefore, focus on the areas of governmental accounting that are different, although we will continue to work with core concepts like the double entry accounting system.

Introduction

In this chapter we will discuss what will be included in the Governmental Accounting. Two hundred capital projects and debt service because we're currently in the overview chapter. As we scroll through the overview we see that we currently have one hundred and eighty four lectures and twenty hours of instructional chapter. This could increase as time passes.

We're not going to go into the cause content chapter. The content will be broken out by chapter heading not every chapter will have the same amount of material within it but the chapter headings will give us a good idea of what will be included within each chapter as we go into each chapter we will typically have an introduction to what the chapter will be covering. We'll have PDA files that will be downloadable. You can use them offline without Internet access. We'll have chapter files that will go over the concepts in a chapter format.

We'll typically have downloadable Excel worksheets along with step by step instructional chapters. The Excel worksheet then can be used to work through a problem and a step by step format. The Excel worksheets typically have three tabs, one tab with the answer to it so you can see how it's all put together. The second tab has a pre formatted worksheet so you can put it together along with step by step instructional chapters, the third tab typically a blank tab that you can format your own Excel worksheets if you so choose.

We generally have multiple choice questions at the end of the chapters as well and an accounting common break to break up the content. And if you go into the next chapter we'll take a look at what will be included in each chapter first we'll have the introduction which will in essence be this. Then we'll go into the governmental accounting overview chapter. This will be kind of a review if you took a look at the prior Book. Government accounting.

One hundred but we want to get back to those core concepts so that we have the core concepts necessary. What is governmental accounting? How do we record governmental accounting? One of the main differences with governmental accounting and for profit accounting and then we'll go into the core concepts that we're working on here capital assets is what we'll start off with what our capital assets are and how they differ in a for profit organization to governmental accounting. How does the recording differ and how might the categories differ between the two?

We will have a lot of similarities as well. We'll take a look at those as well then we'll get into the capital projects fund talking about those long term types of projects so that's one of the major funds we're going to look at here long term projects such as building a bridge and building a free right. Building a road or an overpass. Then we'll take a look at a capital projects fund. The general fund government wide transactions so we'll take a look at example problems as we do so we want to consider the government wide transactions on an accrual basis and on the fund side of things.

The fun side of things often deals with the general fund, one of the main funds and governmental accounting and then Of course the capital project funds so we'll take a look at some examples related to that. We'll take a look at financing sources for capital projects. When we think about capital projects, Of course long term projects like making a building or a bridge need to be financed in some way oftentimes with debt things like issuing bonds is a typical way to finance the capital project. Then we'll take a look at a statement of revenues expenditures and changes in fund balance with relation to the capital project fund.

In other words a financial statement similar to the income statement with regards to a capital project fund which is on a modified accrual basis rather than a normal accrual basis method. Then we'll take a look at the capital project fund and government wide activities transactions. Another example problem with relations to the capital project Fund and the government wide activities the government activities as a whole and then thinking about recording those transactions on the fund level as well for long term projects. Then we'll look at the general long term liabilities and debt service fund overview. So the next fund we want to spend time on is the debt service fund. It deals with long term liabilities so we'll think about our general long term liabilities.

How are they the same or differ from for profit types of organizations in terms of the recording of them, how they're developed, how they're recorded and then the debt service fund which can be used in order to track long term liabilities. Then we'll have the debt service fund general fund capital project fund and government wide transactions. We'll be looking at these transactions as related types of activity that will involve them. When we think about a long term project capital projects that is built in a building or a bridge we'll typically need to find it finance it with bonds or something like that and therefore we'll use the capital project fund possibly have some play with the general fund the main fund and then we've got the government wide transactions recording it on the government level as well. Then we've got these statements of revenues expenditures and changes in fund balance with relation to the debt service fund.

In other words looking at the financial statements similar to the income statement with regards to the debt service fund then we'll go into the debt service fund. Term bonds transactions will go into transactions with relation specifically to the types of bonds of term bonds and then we'll look at the debt service fund capital project and government wide transaction. Another example problem looks at the interplay as we go through the transaction recording them on the government wide level and then the fund level including the capital project Fund and the debt service fund. Then we'll have a comprehensive problem as we've gone through the transaction. So far we've been concentrating on the Capital Projects Fund and the debt service fund as well as the government wide level.

The comprehensive problem will go through a comprehensive problem involving more funds and more of a comprehensive level so we can see the interplay of them as we go. This will typically be in the format of a excel files that we can download which will usually have an answer tab as well as a tab Italy pre formatted that you can fill in the information with and we'll usually have a new worksheet for points along the way so if you wanted to jump to some specific point or rework something within the comprehensive problem you can jump to that Excel worksheet which will start at that point and work through that part.

Governmental Accounting Overview

The governmental accounting overview chapter of the Book will go through an overview of the core concepts for governmental accounting before we get to the specifics that we're concentrating on here which is going to be their capital projects funds and the debt service fund.

Governmental Accounting Objectives

In this chapter we will discuss our objectives for governmental accounting. Our objectives are to make governmental accounting more understandable. Period. There are many obstacles to achieving this objective. One of the obstacles is simply defining what is governmental accounting versus for profit accounting.

What are going to be the differences? What are going to be the similarities and then being able to focus on those differences to be able to better understand them. For example governments like accounting use the same balancing concepts as all accounting. In other words we're gonna be using a double entry accounting system we're going to be using debits and credits. A balancing concept that debits in the credits. However governmental accounting will use many different accounting names then financial accounting. It's going to use different accounting bases often times than a cash basis or an accrual basis as we often know them in financial accounting and it often requires the use of fund accounting which is also a new concept.

One of the problems we have when we move from financial accounting to governmental accounting is to have the idea that we're just going to pick up the same balancing concepts and apply the same double entry accounting system rules to governmental accounting and we'll be able to pick up governmental accounting fairly easily. That's not necessarily the case because there are a substantial amount of differences within governmental accounting and financial accounting. We have to learn these new accounting names. We're going have to learn what the accounting basis will be.

We're going to use fund accounting in other words an understanding of financial accounting and understanding of the double entry accounting system is going to be necessary to fully understand governmental accounting but not necessarily enough to understand governmental accounting because there is going to be substantial new material that will need to understand like many other topics governmental accounting has grown substantially over recent years. And therefore when we think about the curriculum of how we learn governmental accounting it usually hasn't kept pace with the amount of growth within government like counting.

And therefore when we consider governments like counting classes studying for governmental accounting we often have way too much information in one Book or one time of study often combining things like governmental accounting and other nonprofit types of counting too. This would make sense if we think about how accounting has grown over time and how specialized fields have developed over time.

In other words it used to be the case where we would apply double entry accounting concepts to any type of organization for profit government type of organizations. Then we can think about the government organizations and not for profits having different objectives setting up different rules to apply for those different objectives. And Of course as time passes we have more and more differences between the for profit not for profit more regulation and when fields expand rapidly it's usually the case that the curriculum doesn't expand with the growth of the field in relation to the growth of the field so we often end up with situations where we're putting a lot of information into a short amount of time to learn it.

The question then is how can we learn this information more quickly, how can we learn new accounts with different account names more quickly, how can we learn the different accounting bases and when to use them and how to apply fund accounting more quickly. The first thing we will concentrate on here is avoiding floating journal entries. Floating journal entries are going to be the answers to questions when we think about concepts just writing a journal entry and not applying it to anything, not posting it to the goal, not seeing how it relates to a trial balance. This is going to be the typical way that we see answers to questions or how we discuss topics as we get into more advanced accounting classes because most people the professors in those classes the people that write the textbooks expect you to basically be able to visualize the chart of accounts how these things would be posted what the jail would look like what's going to be the effect on net income.

However when we moved to governmental accounting there's a significant amount of changes in terms of the names of the accounts and how these accounts are going to behave and therefore we'd really need to go back to actually posting these items really seeing them being posted so we can see the effect. We'll see an example of this shortly. We will also use a trial balance as much as possible. The trial balance will give us a list of accounts. The grouping of accounts in order in essence assets, liabilities and equity so we can get an idea of these new account names, what types of accounts they are and therefore what the behavior of those accounts will be.

And when we discuss new accounts and journal entries balancing concepts we will post transactions to some type of worksheet so that we can see the end result of a trial balance. Here are a few examples just to get an idea of what we're talking about and what the difference will be. Many times when you look at more advanced accounting topics something like a textbook or a professor will typically just write down the journal entry and if we're thinking about basic accounting concepts this is usually enough we're going to say all we debit this account with credit that account and we have enough visualizations an understanding of a double entry accounting system to be able to grasp what they're saying.

But if we see a journal entry such as this in governmental accounting where we have a debit to something like estimated revenues a credit to appropriations and a debit to the budgetary fund balance that we may look at this and say hey I get that it's in balance but I don't really understand what's happening here this seems very unusual I don't know what any of these accounts are. I don't know how they behave. How can this be more useful? How can we make this easier to do and easier to learn? Well it would be a lot easier if we had something that we were going to post to such as a worksheet if we saw a beginning trial balance and an ending trial balance as we might see in say adjusting type entries a worksheet similar to this. Then we can get a chart of accounts and we can ground ourselves and say OK I may not know still what a budgetary fund balance is but I can see where this is being posted to I can see the behavior of the starting point the change and the ending point within this worksheet that can give me some context at least to start with.

As we go forward and understand this I could see that we started with something in balance. We then did something that's going to be in balance in terms of debits and credits. We ended with something in balance that could give us some context. I may not know what appropriations are but I can see them down here in like the temporary accounts. What would be the income statement accounts in a for profit type of organization that can at least give me some context. We can go from there and pick up that information much more easily if we see it and visualize it in this format.

Something that we can't do even if we understand financial accounting when we move to governmental accounting because we can't visualize these accounts. We've never seen them and we haven't worked with them a lot before. The same is going to be true with the estimated revenues being basically in essence posting like budget type accounts here. So we have estimated revenues. It's difficult for us to visualize what that will be like if we have a chart of accounts and a worksheet that's going to be much easier for us to do. Another example is if we saw a journal entry like this and someone was just going to explain this journal entry Well we debit and conferences and we credit and conferences outstanding.

We can talk about that and we can start to visualize that but it's very difficult for us to see it in context because these are two accounts that we wouldn't have no one we don't really understand for financial accounting and conferences I don't know what that is I don't have a grasp of what that is might help if we saw that account related to other accounts and actually posted the transaction to something like a worksheet and at least then we could see Okay assets liabilities something similar to equity accounts something similar to income statement or timing and type accounts. This has given me a more of a grasp that we can start from and then I can say okay encumbrances outstanding is in this kind of area which I would compare to in financial accounting to equity.

So it's going to be something different for governmental accounting but I could start to relate these concepts much more easily. If we if we don't just have the floating journal entry but we actually post them to something like a worksheet in conferences is down here I still may not know exactly what it is but I can see OK it's down here in what I would expect to be more income statement type of accounts because they were there in the income statement location that I would expect for for profit.

And then again I'm not we're not going to go into the details here about these journal entries but just that's the idea that we're going to get some more more context than we typically would with most Books most Books are just going to give you the journal entry and then expect you to basically visualize everything else which we can't really do because governmental accounting is substantially different.

Governmental Accounting vs Not-For-Profit Accounting

In this chapter we will compare governmental accounting vs. not for profit accounting. First question you might have is aren't they the same thing because oftentimes we see these things grouped together if we see a Book in government or accounting we typically see governmental accounting not for profit accounting grouped together and the answer to that is that it depends when we think about the governmental and not for profit and we compare that to the grouping of the for profit that's just going to be one format that we can group information together is just like grouping anything else together is the same kind of ideas grouping something like a cap to something like a tiger we might say well they're both in the category of cats but if we wanted to study one or the other or group them into one Book of study we would probably want to separate the two because there's enough distinction between them at this point in time that we would want to focus in on them individually at one point in time they were probably much the same and we could study them together without any type of problem the same is gonna be true with different formats and different specializations within business within accounting at one point in time all of accounting was basically covered by the double entry accounting system.

That's it as time passes then more specialization happens such as governmental accounting breaking off and basically being a subfield that we have to think about separately because there's enough difference to do so and then we have the governmental and not for profit which at this point in time that's a lot of information. So we probably want to break those two out and think of them separately. One to point that out here for a few different reasons.

One Of course is just so that we have them distinct in our mind. So we know what these groupings mean and how we want to approach them and study them so we want to know what we're thinking about when we want to understand a certain concept. So in other words if you're here for something like a not for profit and you run something like a small not for profit type of organization then you might be overwhelmed if you start thinking about and comparing to governmental accounting which is going to use fund accounting.

We may not need fund accounting although some of the not for profit type concepts might apply to other smaller nonprofit types of organizations. If on the other hand we're studying accounting for some formalized studies such as a CPA exam then we typically end up grouping the not for profits and profits together and concentrate a lot of our time on the Governmental Accounting because that's often the one that's going to have the most regulations and oftentimes most complexities therefore including things like fund accounting. If we're a small not for profit organizations then many times we can think about some of the concepts and the objectives of the accounting being similar but oftentimes many of the concepts such as fund accounting may not be applicable to the not for profit organizations and it might be a little bit overwhelming to consider all the rules for governmental accounting when we're thinking about I'm not for profit accounting we'll take a look at that in a bit more detail shortly.

First we want to look at how these things are going to be similar to why we have grouped them together not for profits and governmental accounting. One way we can think about these groupings and subgroups of accounting is to consider governmental accounting compared to for profit accounting. In other words if we think about accounting fields in general and how they have developed the accounting Dublin accounting system would be applied to all types of organizations and then at some point in time as things grow as more regulations happen we break out and consider because of different objectives the Government and not for profits breaking out separately from the for profit. So we have the for profits now being substantially distinct then the not for profit to the point where we consider them two different areas we're going to consider them two different fields of study to some degree obviously there's a lot of overlap and then there's going to be some differences given the changes that have taken place.

What then is the root cause or the key component that defines the changes between a for profit organization and accounting for it and the government and non for profit basically stems from this concept. The for profit organization the owners which we would think of as stockholders if it's a corporation expect a return on investment proportional to resources provided in other words if we're the owner of an organization we're putting our time or money into that organization and we expect to get a return direct return on what we have put into that organization and therefore we are going to be regulating that we're going to be making sure that we measure the performance of the organization to see that we are getting a return that means that the stockholders of the organization are really the primary people that check whether or not that organization is achieving their objectives because they expect to have that market pressure that market return on the investment that they have put into the organization.

Both government and not for profit organizations are financed by providers who do not expect benefits proportional to the resources they provide. So in other words if we think about an organ government type of organization they're going to get resources in terms of tax dollars in order to pay for necessary things. But people in pain in the tax dollars aren't looking for a director's return. They're not expecting a direct return. And the same type of way that you'll have that direct return with a for profit type of organization. Therefore the oversight is a little bit more difficult to see because the people that are putting the money in are not regulating in the same way that you would think that would happen for a for profit organization because you don't have that direct return type of relationship.

The same thing happens with a charitable organization. We put money into a charitable organization to save for medical resources or care in some way or a church or something like that. They take those resources and use it towards some type of goal, however that goal isn't a direct return to the people that are giving the money into the organization and therefore the oversight that the people would typically have in a for profit organization. In other words at a for profit organization we're going to monitor very closely the performance of how management is doing because we expect that direct return when we don't expect that direct return. There's less monitoring when we donate to a charity.

We may not spend as much of our time determining whether or not there is a return. That's not going directly to us but to other people. And therefore the accounting for the organization needs to be in some ways more transparent. It's actually more difficult in some ways because we don't have that market pressure that we would have in the for profit organization. The other way we can group the government and not for profit organizations together and compare and contrast them for it to a for profit organization is through the tax code. We can basically say well a for profit organization is going to be subject to taxation.

The profits are going to be subject to taxation. The government and not for profit organizations are often exempt from taxes. So that's gonna be another way that we can define government and not for profit being grouped together as opposed to for profit being subject to taxes not for profit oftentimes not being subject to taxes. Obviously if we're thinking about something like the government they're not going to tax themselves it would be kind of redundant to tax themselves we tax other organizations.

The tax is the revenue to the government. That's not going to be something that they typically pay if they're going to be the receivers. That's one way we can consider that one where we can define a not for profit organization something like a charity is to simply say that they qualify for tax exemption in some way in some way they're not going to be paying the tax in the same way as a for profit type of organization because they qualify under the tax code for some type of exemption. That's another way that we can define and group and not for profit and governmental together as compared and composed to the for profit organization.

Now let's take a look at some of the regulations as we compare them to our three basic categories that we have. We've got the for profit organizations, we have the not for profit organizations and we have the governmental types of organizations. And this is going to be the type of regulations that we have. We have the FSB which is the Financial Accounting Standards Board. Note that for profits are gonna be subject to FAS the government is subject to fast as well as not for profit. And you can think of this as being similar to weight to the way accounting is basically grown up and how it has evolved. In essence it is being applied to all types of organizations. That's where the basic accounting principles start. Then the regulation happens with FASB as it applies it to standard accounting.

Typically concerned with for profit types of organizations but also flying double entry accounting to governmental and not for profit. And then as things evolved so do the regulations right. So then we have Gatsby Governmental Accounting Standards and this is gonna be where we can think of the evolution happening and we say OK we've realized that there are some areas that the FASB is normal accounting that has different concepts that are necessary and therefore different regulations that are necessary.

Gatsby then is going to be an added type of regulation to fill in those places where the FSB doesn't isn't adequate for governmental accounting. And then we have the FDA as a body which is the Federal Accounting Standards Advisory Board and then it applies to the federal government and its agencies and departments. So you can see here that even if we compare the not for profit to the governmental type of organizations that governmental type of organizations have a lot more regulations that we have to comply with and therefore as these things grow we want to probably break out the not for profit and think of them even separately as the governmental type of organizations.

Given the fact that we're going to have a lot more to deal with as the governmental organizations apply these different types of regulations when one of the major differences between them not for profit organization and governmental organizations is that it's less likely that the not for profit organization will have to apply full fund accounting although they might have other things that they must do to track things differently than a for profit types of organization that governmental accounting is more likely to use full fund accounting which is going to be a system that can be a bit complex.

Does Non-Profit Mean Money Does Not Matter

In this chapter we will take a look at the question of does not for profit mean that money doesn't matter for a not for profit type organization. This can seem like a silly question especially when we're talking about the accounting for a not for profit organization but terms like not for profit can't be taken out of context can be a little bit confusing when we compare and contrast them to for profit types of organizations. So the answer to the question does it not for profit mean that money doesn't matter to a not for profit organization.

I'm going to say no. And then we might ask well why does money matter if the objective of a not for profit organization is theoretically not for profit. And the reason money matters whether it be for profit or not for profit is because that's gonna be our major measuring tool. That's what we're doing within the accounting department. We're trying to measure the performance of how well whatever the objective of the organization is they are doing within it. The dollar is going to be our measuring tool, it's going to be our ruler in order to look at the similarities and the differences.

Let's consider the accounting equation when we think of the accounting equation we think about assets liabilities and equity for a for profit organization we typically see the assets. That's what the company has minus the liabilities that the company owes. That's gonna be loans accounts payable, other types of notes payable and then we have the equity. And this is the value of the organization. And Of course the organization is owned by the owners. And therefore this would be the net value to the owners of the organization so the owners then have an objective to regulate how the assets are used and how the liabilities are leveraged in order to hopefully increase the value or equity of the organization.

The double entry accounting system for a not for profit organization or governmental organization will be much the same and that will still have assets will still have liabilities obligations and the difference between the two. We're gonna call something like net position but in essence we have the same thing as equity. The difference between the two is that the equity represents typically the value to the owner whereas the net position because we don't have a particular owner that can claim value of the net position the net position is the net worth the assets over the liabilities that can be used in the future in order to achieve whatever the objective of the organization is. That could be a charitable type of organization or whatever the services that need to be rendered from the governmental type of organization. Therefore the measuring of these resources are gonna be measured in terms of dollars we're going to use dollars to measure assets, liabilities and the net value of the organization.

The for profit organization is going to be heavily regulated by the market by the owner of the company. If it's a publicly traded company we're talking about stockholders of the organization. And if we're talking about a governmental or not for profit organization we still need to measure this stuff and even be more transparent with the information the money matters more or the measurement matters more. In some ways we want to make it as transparent as possible because we don't have these owners that are going to be as vigilant and take a look at the measuring tools and the objectives being achieved within the organization through that profit objective.

Over here we don't have the profit objective and therefore the people that are donating to the organization aren't going to be the people that are benefiting from the net position or at least not directly. So in other words the people that are donating to a charity or the people paying taxes may get benefits from the charity or from the services that a government organization might provide. But they're not getting the direct benefit that's in proportion to what they're giving in terms of the taxes or the donation as they would expect to have.

With regards to a for profit organization therefore the money in terms of measuring with the money is often more important to be really transparent as possible given the fact that we have less market pressure to meet and to make sure that that money is being managed as well as possible. Another way to consider this is with the income statement type accounts where we have revenue minus expenses giving us a for profit net income. So when we think about a for profit type of organization in terms of performance, how are they doing we think about the income statement we think about how much revenue they are generating, how much expenses they had to take in order to generate that revenue and then the net income is what increases the value of the equity of the organization.

And that would be something that the owner would be very concerned with the stockholders and in a publicly traded company because that's going to increase the value directly relational to the owners in a governmental or not for profit organization. We still have revenue but the revenue is going to be from donors or taxpayers or something like that. We still have expenses but note that for a for profit organization we can basically think of those expenses as something that we needed to consume in order to achieve the goal of new generation when we think about the expenses for a not for profit organization it may not have as good as much of a link that the expenses are going to be related to the generation of revenue as they would be for the goal of the organization to achieve whatever objectives social objective of the organization.

But however the difference between revenue and expenses will still give us the other revenue over the expenses. In essence the same type of net income type of calculation and those resources the revenue over the expenses would be something that we can then increase what would be similar to the equity chapter or the assets minus the liability. What we can then use in order to achieve the goals and objectives of the organization. So it's still going to be necessary for us Of course. Probably even more necessary for us to concentrate more and be more transparent once again in terms of what the revenues are, what the expenses are, and how we're extending this money.

The fact that the expenses are not tied to simply the goal of revenue generation makes it a little bit more difficult for us to determine whether or not those expenses are going to be worthwhile for us to be extending in as opposed to for a for profit organization. The expenses are geared towards the generation of revenue. We have a specific goal and we have owners that are really vigilant in terms of whether or not these expenses are achieving that objective of revenue generation.

Over here we're saying we have expenses that may not be tied directly to the revenue generation. So we have to be more transparent to be able to see where this and where these expenses are going so that we can better make decisions about it. So obviously measuring these items is very important to also note that when we think about these expense items we can also consider who is benefiting from the revenue and the money that's going through these types of organizations.

Clearly when we think of a for profit organization we consider the revenue minus the expenditures that go in. In essence to the owner or the owners value then increasing. So we could see directly that the bottom line of the income statement is benefiting the owner. When we consider the organization in terms of a not for profit or governmental organization we see the bottom line as basically increasing the value to the organization. But it's not being applied directly to a specific type of owner.

However we also have within both of these types of organizations included in these expenses things such as wages. So when we consider the money that's being used we have to consider the expenses the value of these expenses and make sure that those are going to be valued well because with it with whatever organization we're thinking about those expenses are gonna be regulated on the for profit side by market pressure to see if they're justified in order to generate revenue.

The expenses with a governmental or not profit organization don't have the same type of market pressure. So determining what these expenses should be can be a little bit more difficult. And Of course included in those expenses are wages. So a substantial amount of people Of course make their money from or earn a living through working for not for profit and governmental organizations. And we need to be able to measure and make sure we're as transparent as possible to decide the proper types of expenses and how they're being expensed. And so.

So these are the types of people that Of course are going to be concerned with the allocation of resources because to the governmental organization it's expenses to the organizations but to these individuals to the workers of the audit organization it is revenue to them. So we want to make sure that Of course that calculation of that revenue the application of the revenue is indeed important.

Governmental Accounting Objectives

In this chapter we will take a look at Governmental Accounting objectives as we go into the Governmental Accounting objectives. We first want to look at the structure of Governmental Accounting and compare it to the structure of financial accounting so we can take what we know from financial accounting.

Apply it to where it does apply to governmental accounting and then consider those areas where the Governmental Accounting differs why it would differ what's going to be the effect on the objectives and then the procedures with regards to those differences or as a result of them. When we think about the governmental accounting structure we think where should the power ultimately lie. Similarly to with a for profit type of organization you would think kind of with the owners for a for profit organization with a governmental organization.

You would think with the people that people are the people that should have control ultimately how through voting teams so the public votes for people to be representatives in the government and those people their representatives then should make decisions on behalf of the people. That's pretty similar to financial accounting actually. Would you say a publicly traded company, let's say, is going to be the shareholders? The shareholders then vote for the people to be on the Board of Directors, the Board of Directors hiring, then management to have the day to day type decision processes.

So as we think think about the government's like counting we can't compare and contrast it to basically the structure of a large type of company in that the owners are basically a step removed in some ways because the owners are the ones that are going to benefit ultimately but they're actually voting for people to be representing them in some way either in the board of directors or within governments like counting people that will be the decision makers government agencies and organizations will take a typically be empowered and accountable to higher levels of government. So that's going to be our system of controls which are typically going to have these checks and balances and we're gonna have the governmental agencies that are going to be over sought by other types of governmental agencies in order to keep those governmental agencies accountable.

Note this is going to be really important because the owners, unlike for a for profit type of organization within a governmental type of organization, aren't expecting a direct return in terms of their investment. So although ultimately the power should be in the people in terms of the governmental organization and in terms of the owners for a for profit type of organization the for profit type organization probably is going to have more market pressure and oversight.

The people that vote for the board of directors having a direct need or a direct desire to have a return on the investment whereas the people here when we think about the people in terms of voting for legislation and for government aren't expected net direct returns more indirect and therefore we have to have some system of control some sets of controls that are a bit different possibly than a for profit organization more transparent possibly than a for profit organization. And Of course we also have within the government the power of taxation. So that's going to be a major form of revenue to the government that's going to be different than a for profit type of organization.

And Of course who the taxes are going to be applied to. They're going to be applied to the people, the people who are ultimately considered to be in control through the power of the election process. Having this in mind the structure in mind and the comparing and contrasting for profit and governmental type of organizations. Now let's take a look at some specific objectives for financial accounting. Typically includes reliance reliability and comparability.

Remember when we think of a for profit type of organization we're typically thinking of creating the financial statements for external users like investors or creditors and therefore we do want to have a good rechapter of some transparency in terms of the value of the organization that can be reflected in terms of a balance sheet and an income statement. That information has to be relevant and has to be reliable and it has to be comparable to things like prior periods or other types of organizations. That's what's gonna make it most useful to those external users. This is going to be very similar for governmental type of accounting but we also have some more obligations that are going to be designed in governmental type of accounting.

Because of that lack of market pressure most of these will be lined up with more transparency. We want to make sure that governmental accounting is more transparent. Note when we're thinking about financial accounting we're thinking about the investors and we're thinking about the creditors. Usually those people want to know the health of the organization to see whether or not they want to do business with the organization. Do they want to give a loan to the organization or do they want to invest in the organization with governmental accounting. It's not just about whether or not the external users want to do business with the organization and therefore want to know the health of the organization. They want to know the details because we want to know how these resources are being used.

Are they being used in accordance with what's best for what the people deem to be best for society so we can make decisions in terms of voting type of decisions and therefore we typically want to lean towards transparency. We want to have the government's own accounting to be transparent for decision makers to be able to make the judgment as to whether the resources are being allocated efficiently and whether the revenue sources are being drawn as they should in a fair way. Therefore according to Gatsby accountability is the cornerstone of all financial reporting in government and requires governments to justify the raising and use of public resources such as taxes. So they want to justify the raising of them.

Note we're not just trying to see how much revenue is coming in as we might do with a business we're trying to justify those revenues. And that's going to take more transparency in order to make those types of decisions. Obligation to disclose whether current year revenues were sufficient to pay for current year benefits or will future taxpayers be required to pay for them instead. So we want to say hey are the revenues that are coming in sufficient to pay for the obligations that are going out. And if they're not what's going to happen.

Well that means that future taxpayers are gonna be obligated at some point in time. We'll now take a look at objectives that are going to be specific to state and local type governments. Compare actual financial results with legally adopted budgets. So we want to be actually transparent with the budget as well. Who can say hey here's the legally adopted budget here's what actually happened here's how close what actually happened to the adopted budget. Once again being transparent with that type of information we assess financial conditions and results of operations. So what were the conditions? What were the results of the operations?

We want to be able to assist in determining compliance with finance related laws, rules and regulations. Of course we want to be able to see whether or not the organization the state organization was in compliance with laws and regulations and assists in evaluating efficiency and effectiveness. So we want to say "Hey , are they doing their job well?" Are they lean and mean again? Difficult to assess this is a little bit difficult for a governmental type of organization to be kind of as lean and mean as you would think of a for profit organization because of the lack of market pressure because of the lack of the people that are involved the voters having a direct interest in the lean and meanness of the organization have they been able to cut things down to what is necessary to do the job that they're trying to do in terms of a market pressure.

Of course you have the market that forces people to do that or the organization will be run out of the market for governmental type of organizations don't have that same market pressure and therefore in order to see whether or not that the organization is doing their job as well as they can we want to be as transparent as possible so the voters can basically make that determination in one way or another objective specific for the federal governments. So federal government objectives we want to see budgetary integrity so we have that same kind of process of saying here's the budget here's what's actually going to happen. Stewardship.

Are they handling the assets, resources , obligations and power that they're given? Well in accordance with what would be expected by the people and then we have systems of controls that are adequate. Do we have an adequate system of controls within the federal government once again. We don't have that same kind of oversight, that same kind of market pressure. Therefore we're gonna have a bit different type of system of controls that controls similar to a for profit organization because Of course we still want to have that separation of duties and whatnot in a for profit organization in order to catch things like fraud but when we think about governmental organizations especially federal governmental organizations that have a lot of power and control and less oversight or market pressure than we want to make sure that we have a good system of controls between departments so that we have the checks and balance necessary to keep the organizations in line and doing what they should be doing.

Government Financial Reporting Requirements

In this chapter we will take a look at government financial reporting requirements. We're going to start off with the minimum requirements. General Purpose external government financial reporting requirements. They include management's discussion and analysis. This is actually going to be a report of the required supplemental information. This is going to be a key component for the governmental type of organizations because it's designed to give a narrative format an easy to read type format of the basic financial statements and the current financial position and results of financial activities compared to the prior year.

We then have the government wide financial statements and fund financial statements. We'll get more into the difference between the government wide financial statements and fund financial statements. But for now note that the government wide financial statements ought to be focusing in on the entity as a whole the government wide activities focusing in on more of an accrual type standard one that we would be more used to the Fund Financial Statements are going to be breaking things down to relevant components focusing more in on the flows of those relevant components using then a modified accrual type basis oftentimes for the Fund Financial Statements. Then we have the notes to the financial statements and we'd have the required supplemental information.

The key component of the required supplemental information being the management's discussion and analysis focusing on the financial statements. We have the two formats : the government wide financial statements and the Fund Financial Statements. The government wide financial statements give an overview of our government's net position and changes in net position. This can be compared more closely with for profit types of organizations when we're considering. In essence the balance sheet and the income statement we're thinking in essence of the net position balance sheet type activity and the changes in net position income statement.

How did we do performance type of activity over the entire organization which is typically what we would think of in terms of financial statements for a for profit type of organization. Therefore although the terminology will change the government wide financial statements will be more closely related to what we would consider for a for profit type of organization. One of the terms that will change and we'll see more of these as we go is the net position you can consider basically the balance sheet or the accounting equation assets minus liabilities equals equity typically. Well here we can say what the net position is we can think of that as the equity type chapter. Net assets net position assets minus liabilities.

The Fund Financial Statements give more detailed financial information about the government when we compare this to a for profit type of organization. Note that the government wide type statements is what we typically consider because as external users we want to know the organization as a whole to know whether or not we want to do business typically with the organization. That's what we want to see in the financial statements. They fund financial statements to give us more transparency about the operations and what's actually going on.

More detail we're going to pick out the key components and give more detail about those components and therefore the Fund Financial Statements often focus on the short term activity often use modified type accrual methods so that we can see the detail in a more transparent way within the fund accounting government wide financial statements help assess operational accountability whether government has used its assets efficiently and effectively to meet objectives focus on the flow of economic resources and therefore use the typical or standard accrual method that we would expect from financial accounting Fund Financial Statements are a separate set of accounts set up to keep track of resources that have been segregated for a specific purpose.

We'll talk more about how to do that how that process works how we separate this information out in future chapters but just note that when we think about a fund we typically think about a specific purpose that has been set up and a specific set Of courses that are being applied to it and therefore we can consider the fund as in essence a separate type of entity a separate type of entity that is going to be assigned its own set of accounts and therefore have a general ledger and therefore we should theoretically be able to make financial statements from that information and such as a balance sheet type statement a net position type statement and an income statement type statement or a performance type of statement Fund Financial Statements help with fiscal accountability whether the government raised and spent financial resources in accordance with constraints of budget legal and regulations focus on short term flow of current financial resources there's going to be a key component when we think of the fund accounting we're typically thinking about short term flows so this leads us to the use of a modified accrual method rather than a standard type of accrual method so that we'll have slightly different accounting for the funds as a result in part of this focus prepared in conformity with the Cavs PGA SB hundreds Governmental Accounting Standards Board.

Now we're going to talk about a comprehensive annual financial report. This is gonna be over and above the minimum requirements that we have talked about thus far generally not required to prepare the comprehensive annual financial report. The CHF are but most governments do so. The CHF hours are prepared in conformity with Gatsby standards.

The comprehensive annual financial report typically includes an introductory chapter financial chapter a statistical chapter a title page a letter of transmittal and other chapter the financial chapter of the report includes the auditors report that management's discussion and analysis often termed empty and a basic financial statements and related notes required supplementary information that required supplementary information other than the M.D. and A the management's discussion and analysis and other supplementary information. Comprehensive annual financial report statistical chapter typically includes goals and charts showing demographic data, economic data, financial trends and operating information.

Federal Government Financial Reporting Overview

In his chapter he will take a look at an overview of financial reporting for the federal government financial reporting overview. This is going to happen at two levels of the federal government: we have the U.S. government wide and the major agencies and departments U.S. government wide financial reporting prepared by the U.S.

Treasury major agencies and department financial reporting prepared by major agencies and departments in accordance with requirements set in the Office of Management and Budget. The O M B the US government wide consolidated report includes plain language Citizens Guide management's discussion and an analysis to M.D. and A the performance information financial statements supplemental information information both budgetary and proprietary financial activities.

Federal agency and department of financial reporting must prepare a performance and accountability report for the EPA. Ah that includes annual performance report P R annual financial statements and management reports on internal control and other accountability issues.

State & Local Governmental Accounting Objectives, Primary Users,

In this chapter we will take a look at state and local governmental accounting objectives. Primary users and usefulness starting with objectives provide information that can be used to assess a government's accountability. Recall that accountability being the cornerstone of Governmental Accounting assists users in making economic, social and political decisions.

This objective being substantially different than a for profit organization where typically we're thinking about the users being external users people like creditors and investors thinking about doing business with the organization here. We're talking about the users making decisions related to economic social decisions and political decisions. That difference in objective often results in accounting practices and rules generally with the idea of more transparency. The objective of giving more transparent data and information so people can make these types of decisions.

Now we'll talk about the concept of usefulness with regards to state and local governmental accounting. Some of these will look familiar with rich objectives for for profit organizations and some of them will be added to those objectives first being understandable the financial statements the accounting needs to be understandable this is going to be really important for governmental accounting because unlike with financial accounting when we're thinking about the external users we're thinking about investors and creditors probably have some familiarity with the types of regulations for putting these resources together and working with financial statements specific to their investment or credit type engagements.

When we're thinking about governmental accounting however we're dealing with financial statements that may be given to citizens who may not have as much understanding in terms of financial transactions financial statements the Governmental Accounting being a bit different in terms of the objectives Of course different governmental accounting units having different objectives fund accounting being a bit different and therefore there's gonna be I need to make sure that the financial statements are transparent. That's going to be one of the objectives we want to have to have everything out there but also understandable which is going to be an added challenge given the differences with accounting.

The broad range of governmental accounting and the needs that are out there as well as the users who are using the financial statements. Then we have to be reliable . We have to be able to depend on the numbers. We have to have faith and trust that the numbers have been put together correctly in accordance with some set of standards. We need to have timely information. We can't have financial statements that are too old because then they're not going to be useful anymore. So the financial data has to be compiled in some type of timely fashion and be presented so that it will be useful to the users. The financial statements note that reliability and timely are two concepts that we'll see and for profit types organizations in terms of typical objectives for financial accounting.

Consistency is another concept that will typically be seen with for profit organizations in that we want to make sure that whatever principles you use are consistent. If we're applying an accrual method to one set Of courses we want to apply it to the next time period. If we're applying a modified accrual we want to be consistent. We want to be able to compare this year to last year we want to be able to use and to do so we need to use the same kind of accounting bases the same methods the same set of rules the same set of standards and we want to have comparability. Again this is something you'll see in objectives for for profit types of organizations.

We need to have comparability and consistency in comparability linked together in many ways because Of course to have consistency will help us to have comparability between different types of governmental units would be nice to be able to compare state to state type of information. It would also be nice to compare. We want to be able to compare prior time periods and want to compare the current period to the prior period. How can we have comparability?

We have some kind of standardization. We have some kind of set of rules and we have consistency with the application of those standards so that the financial statements are going to be standardized in a way that we can compare them to prior periods to other areas to other financials.

State & Local Governmental Accounting Supplemental Information

In this chapter we will discuss state and local governmental accounting supplemental information in a prior chapter. We discussed minimum requirements for general purposes external governmental financial reporting amongst those minimum requirements were the supplemental information. Now we're gonna go into a little bit more depth in terms of what the supplemental information is required supplemental information also termed R as it is used to provide essential information and note that some of this information in the required supplemental information is considered to be essential.

That's why it's going to be required supplemental information; the financial statements and related notes would not be presented in the correct context without the RSI the required supplemental information. So once again it is a requirement for the minimum requirements primary examples of are as I required supplementary information are the management discussion and analysis. This is the first thing that should really come to mind because this is going to put that narrative format of the objectives and this is gonna be something that's considered very necessary within the chapter of the governmental type of activities to get common users an idea of the financial statement information as well as an outline of what the objectives are and then we have the budget to actual schedules and pension disclosures.

Then we have other supplementary information as opposed to required supplementary information. The other supplementary information is useful but not essential to understanding the financial statement and notes often found in the statistical chapter of the comprehensive annual financial reports the CHF are and recall that the CHF are not required but often put together by the state and local governments. In other words the CHF hours above and beyond the minimum requirements. But it's becoming more and more standardized and something that more state governments do.

State & Local Governmental Accounting Elements of Financial

In his chapter we will discuss state and local government accounting elements of financial statements elements of financial statements before an item is allowed to be recognized. It must meet the definition of an element. These elements will look familiar. They'll basically be breaking out the balance sheet and income statement type accounts that we'll be considering basically account classes we're considering the accounting equation.

In essence Assets Liabilities Equity and in the income statement where for a for profit would be revenue and expenses. So we're considering kind of like the equivalent of these categories which we're going to list out as elements. So let's list out those elements and define them. There are seven elements. These are the seven elements starting with acid resources with present service capacity that the government presently controls. Then we have deferred outflows of resources and the consumption of net assets by the government. That applies to a future reporting period. And then we have liabilities and present obligations to sacrifice the resources that the government has little or no discretion to avoid. Then we have deferred inflows of resources and the acquisition of net assets by the government. That applies to a future reporting period.

Then we have a net position residual when assets plus deferred outflows minus liabilities minus deferred inflows is calculated. Net position appears in a statement of financial position. This would be equivalent to an equity for a for profit balance sheet which would be equivalent to the net position which would appear on the statement of financial positions the statement of financial positions being similar to a balance sheet for a for profit organization. Then we have what we would consider more income statement type accounts which is an inflow of resources. The acquisition of net assets by the government in the current reporting period. Examples. Revenue and other resources.

And then we have an outflow of resources. What we would consider the expense type portion or similar to an expense type portion for a for profit. And that would be the consumption of net assets by the government in the current reporting period. Examples include expenses, expenditures depending on if we're on an accrual or modified accrual basis and other uses of resources. So here we have our equation in terms of our accounting equation. You'll recall the accounting equation assets equal Liabilities plus equity we're going to convert that to the format of assets minus liabilities equals equity and then we're dealing with these other two components which are going to be added to basically our equation.

So you'll note here we have assets now. So we have assets rather than current assets which we'll discuss in terms of fund accounting financial statements where when we think about a fund we're thinking about current flows typically. So we have assets here plus deferred outflows. These are gonna be items that are going to increase the fund balance as assets do but don't qualify specifically in the same category of assets. Then we're going to subtract out the liabilities and we also have the deferred inflows the deferred inflows like the deferred outflows are in and like the liabilities are going to decrease the fund balance similar to a liability but can't be categorized as the same definition of liabilities.

And then that's going to be equivalent to the fund balance which you could think of as kind of the equity chapter and you'll recall that you want to know these terms in terms of the fund balance if you hear something like net assets if you see something like equity. These are all kind of conceptually the same, it just depends on the type of organization entity that we're talking about. So for profit entities a sole proprietor typically called owners equity a partnership Partnership's equity. If we're talking about a corporation shareholder's equity, if we're talking about other types of entities that might be called net position fund balance they're all gonna be named for that basically assets minus liabilities equals that net position fund balance equity type of chapter.

So we have a similar accounting equation assets minus liabilities but we're gonna break out these components deferred outflows and deferred inflows which are going to act like in essence assets and liabilities a component of assets and liabilities but don't technically fall into the asset class and the liability class and therefore are going to be broken out into their own chapters when we consider basically the balance sheet and the accounting equation for it.

State & Local Governmental Accounting Financial Reporting Model

In this chapter we will take a look at state and local governmental accounting and financial reporting models. Our general model is that we will have the basic financial statements and we'll have the government wide activity and then we will have the fund activity. We'll have the government wide financial statements. We'll have the Fund Financial Statements activities of governments are typically broken out into the categories of business type activities governmental activities and fiduciary activities.

When we think about the different types of funds will typically follow this kind of grouping model as we group the types of funds that will be set up business type activities are going to be similar to a for profit type of organization where we might think that there's some type of customers involved in the process. Governmental activities are some type of service type of activity for the government and fiduciary activities. Thinking about a trust or some type of holding activity for the government where they have a fiduciary responsibility for government wide financial statements.

Now we're focusing on the government wide as opposed to the Fund Financial Statements have a measurement focus of economic resources and therefore they're going to be using an accrual basis. They're gonna be using an accrual basis as opposed to a modified accrual. Accountability will be operational. The government wide financial statements have a statement of net position reports at year end financial position. The statement of net position is Of course very similar to what we would think of as a balance sheet.

Where do we stand at a particular point in time where you have different types of terminology statement of net position because Of course we're going to name some of the accounts, especially the equity chapter for a for profit organization differently for a governmental organization. But we have the same kind of accounting equation or a similar type of an accounting equation where we would have assets minus liabilities equals equity or in this case the net position you might hear a term net assets. We typically are going to use net position in the state governmental accounting. So in essence balance sheet where do we stand at a particular point in time.

Statement of activity reports expenses and revenues classified by program or function. And this Of course would be similar to the statement or an income statement we're to show the activity the performance over time expenses and revenue notice we're using an accrual basis and therefore have the term expenses rather than something like expenditures when we're considering the government wide financial statement used as separate columns columns for governmental activities business type activities and component units. So we're going to break out those into separate columns for the governmental activity business type activities and component units Fund Financial Statements will typically be grouped into government type funds proprietary funds and Fiduciary Funds.

The government funds are gonna be the largest grouping of different funds for different services of the government. The proprietary funds are going to be those activities where we have something similar to a for profit organizations such as customers and therefore can account for these funds on more of it and accrual type basis and the fiduciary is where the government's going to have a fiduciary type of responsibility when we consider the government funds we're talking about fiscal accountability is going to be our focus.

Flow of current financial resources. Notice that our focus here is on current financial resources and therefore we're going to use a modified accrual. So for most of the funds that we're going to set up we're going to think about when we set up a fund. Most of the funds we set up will be government funds. Therefore the focus is gonna be on current financial resources and therefore we're gonna be using a modified accrual basis as opposed to the government wide activities where we use the accrual basis. Then we have the proprietary funds and the proprietary funds are gonna be those that are similar to a for profit organization they function in essence more like a sole proprietor or a for profit type of organization in that we have something like customers and therefore our focus is operational accountability flow of economic resources and therefore we use the accrual basis.

So this is going to be more similar when we think of proprietary funds of what we would expect for a for profit type of organization using an accrual basis in essence because it's functioning in a similar fashion as a for profit organization. Given the fact that we have that for profit type of nature possibly having customers that we're charging for some types of goods or services and then we have the fiduciary fund where we might have some kind of holding or trust type fund a fiduciary type activity you can't imagine something like a donation to a governmental fund where you can't touch the actual principal but the interest on it is something that can be used or something like that.

We have the fiduciary activity that is going to have an operational accountability flow of economic resources and also using the accrual basis. So once again overview typically considering funds most of the funds will be grouped up here. Government type funds and use that modified accruals. That's where your default wants to be and then we'll have those types of funds that could be proprietary or fiduciary when those are in place when they're applicable. And those types of funds will be using what would be more familiar with the accrual basis. Government funds will have a balance sheet, a statement of revenues expenditures and changes in fund balance. And notice when we consider these financial statements remember we have the government wide activities and then the funds are broken out in their own set Of courses, their own set of general ledgers and therefore we can create their own financial statements with them when we consider the governmental type funds.

We have a balance sheet. We have a statement of revenues expenditures and changes in fund balance. Long way to say this is kind of the equivalent of the income statement but you'll note that it's gonna be because it is on the modified accrual type basis we have expenditures here and there's going to be a different basically accounting method for it but in essence Of course we have the position statement and balance sheet where we added a certain point in time and the activity statement. How have we done over a given time frame starting and ending point? Statement of revenues expenditures and changes in fund balance in the proprietary funds we have the statement of net position balance sheet type of account and in the statement of revenues expenses and changes in fund.

Net position again income statement type of account closer to what we would expect like an income statement because we have the term expenses here rather than expenditures indicating an accrual method as opposed to a modified accrual method being used above. And then a statement of cash flows and then we have the fiduciary fund which has a statement of fiduciary net position and a statement of change in fiduciary net position. Again same kind of activity or thought process there Of course where do we stand at a point in time.

What has happened over a certain time frame. Governmental Accounting reconciliation due to governmental activities being reported using the accrual basis and the government wide financial statements of remember that government wide financial statements used the accrual basis but reporting using a modified accrual basis and in the governmental funds financial statements. So we have a different method being used for the government wide and then we break out the fund activities.

We're using a different method accrual versus a modified accrual fund balance and operating results on the fund balance. Financial statements must be reconciled to those presented on the government wide financial statements. So due to this difference due to these two methods being used we need to have a reconciliation process between the two.

State & Local Governmental Accounting Fund Reporting

In this chapter we will focus on fund reporting for state and local governmental accounting. First we'll think about why the funds developed and what the funds are. Once we have a little bit of history on why the funds developed we might be able to have a better idea of what the funds currently are how they're going to be used and possibly more incentive to learn about the fund accounting fund reporting developed to meet the needs of reporting revenues and related expenditures that are legally or contractually constrained for specific purposes separately from revenues and expenditures.

Without these constraints you can imagine the need that's going to be developed. We're saying okay there's gonna be some legal or contractual constraint for these funds. How are we going to track the fact that there's some type of legal or contractual restraint for these funds. We could set up some type of fund account in separating this information out in some way somehow earmarking it or somehow putting a tag on these revenues and these expenses and relating them together in some format and you could see how that would develop into some type of system.

The system being in our case fund accounting fund reporting the concept of a fund in other words what is a fund. A fund is a separate fiscal entity which means it has its own resources, its own liabilities and operating activities has its own set of accounting records that allow it to prepare separate financial statements. Therefore a fund is a separate accounting entity. In other words the fund we can think of is similar to a business type of entity, even a sole proprietor having a separate set Of courses that's going to be our fundamental principle.

We want to basically separate the books from the owners set Of course so the personal books should be separated from the entities books even with regards to a sole proprietor where we don't have the business being a separate legal entity. We still have a separate set Of courses in that case with regards to a C Corporation. Remember we have actually a separate legal entity in actual the ownership would be separate but in essence we want to set up a separate set Of courses. Similar concept is gonna be here with the funds. We're going to say Alright this is gonna be a particular fund we're gonna set up a separate basically accounting entity a separate set Of courses for it those set Of courses having their own general ledgers and therefore we can create the financial statements from that accounting information fund categories. These are going to be the categories that we're going to group these different types of funds into governmental funds.

This is going to be typically the largest category that we'll have. So when we think about different types of funds we are usually considering a governmental type fund. Most of the time we have proprietary funds proprietary funds are going to be those that act more like a business type of activity where we might have some type of customer type of relationship or similar to a customer type of relationship within those types of funds so they behave differently and then we have the fiduciary funds where the fund has some type of fiduciary responsibility we'll get into some more detail about these categories now.

Now we'll look at the governmental funds category. This is the largest category of the three right. We have these three categories. Now we're looking at the governmental funds. The largest category, the governmental funds, will include the general fund. The general fund is the most important fund that we're going to have. Now consider this we're going to have fund accounting that's going to be different from the government wide reporting. We've got the government wide reporting that we're going to have and then we've got the fund accounting and then we have the general fund which is going to be like the overarching type of fund. In other words any type of fund accounting system is going to have a general fund or something could be named something differently but a general fund type of fund is going to be applicable. Every accounting system will have a general fund and every system will only have one general fund.

So that's going to be distinct and different from the other fund we're going to be like the most important fund Of course. For that reason other funds might have multiple different funds depending on the needs of the government so we may have none of them. We may have multiple funds in others in some of these other types of categories. We'll have this special revenue fund. A special revenue fund will be set up if we have a grant or some type of gift that is given and it's for a specific type of purpose. So let's say we have a grant or a gift and that is going to be restricted for the maintenance and use of a building or a fountain. Then we might set up a special revenue fund to be able to track that debt service fund.

Governments that have bond obligations outstanding and certain other types of long term general liabilities may be required to create a debt service fund. The reason for the debt service fund is to account for financial resources segregated for making principal and interest payments on general long term debt that we have the capital projects funds. So a government might put and set up capital projects such as building a bridge or building a building and in order to track the funds related to the capital project we would set up a capital project fund. Typically thinking about a long term type of project that we're going to have and wanting to account for that capital project in a separate fund.

And Of course note that we might have multiple capital project funds going on at the same time because we might have different capital projects and we want to track that information in different funds. Then we have the fund balance classification. The fund balance is kind of like the equity chapter so when we consider the balance sheet or the accounting equation we could consider assets minus liabilities equals what would be the equity chapter for for profit organization fund balance here. When we consider the fund balance for a for profit that is the amount that we would allocate to the owner.

The net value of the business is the same for a governmental organization or the fund. The fund assets minus the liabilities is the fund balance. When we consider the fund balance then we're also considering the fact that people are going to want to appropriate those funds or assign those funds and want to use those funds in some way and we want to be as transparent as possible. So when we consider government accounting and people are looking at these Fund Financial Statements each of these funds having their own financial statement they're going to be looking at.

Okay, here's the assets minus the liabilities. Here's the fund balance. I want to do something with that fund balance. I want to use it in some way. I want to apply it in some way. I want that money some way right and we're going to have to assign those funds in some way. Well that being the case we're going to want to identify different categories of the fund balances and say there's different levels of restrictions to the fund balance.

Now the levels of restriction can get a bit complicated because there's a lot of different levels of restriction but the concept note what we're basically saying hey this is the fund balance. This is the difference between the assets and the liabilities. People want this money in some way. They want to assign it out in some way. We need to have if there's any restriction on these balances to note some type of level of restrictions so people know whether or not they can possibly get access to this money in some way. So the restrictions that we have from highest to lowest are non-spend. So if we say the fund balances are non-spendable in some way we're just saying hey it's you know that is included in the fund balance assets minus liabilities are there but don't expect to get it because it's totally restricted it's non spendable for four.

And we'll talk more about as we go through problems what it means to be non spendable but the second level will be restricted then. So then you have a little bit greater likelihood but possibly not going to get access to the fund balance act there. The next level is committed, the next level is assigned, the next level is unassigned. So when we're considering the fund balance are we gonna be able to get use of the fund balance we want to think about these levels of restriction in terms of the fund balance and Of course when we report the financial statements that's going to be one of the things we have to consider in terms of the Fund Financial Statements when we consider what would be the equity chapter we have to then think about how we're going to break out the equity chapter to the various assignments of of the fund balance classifications is the fund balance non spendable restricted committed assigned or unassigned reporting major funds.

Gatsby requires separate columns for major funds. So therefore we have to identify what the major funds are going to be and then we have to have a separate column for the reporting of the major funds. Non major funds may be grouped together and reported in one column. So the idea here Of course being that when we think about governmental accounting we want to be as transparent as possible so people have the information they need. But we know that most people don't really care. I mean most people are still looking at the government's old books as a whole. And the smaller funds aren't something that they really are going to need the detail in. Therefore it's not required to break them out.

Oftentimes we want to break out what would be considered the major funds and then possibly group together the minor funds in one column general fund general funds and funds meeting both of the following are going to be the items that are going to be the major funds that we have to group out Total Assets Liabilities revenues or expenditures expenses of the fund are at least 10 percent or the corresponding element total for all funds of that category or type. And the same element that met the 10 percent criterion is at least 5 percent or the corresponding element total for all governmental and enterprise funds combined. So in essence we have this very specific category that will tell us whether or not we have to sign out and break out into its own column a specific major fund reporting non major funds even though Gatsby's requires non major funds to be reported in a single column.

Many governments report details regarding Don major funds separately, often combining financial statements as part of the C A F R or the comprehensive annual financial report. In essence then we have a very stringent requirement for the requirement to break out the major funds. The idea being that we want to be as transparent as possible with the major categories that people are going to need and want to see but not be too detailed. And that's what's going to be required to be reported however reported in the comprehensive annual financial report.

Remember that this isn't even required at all the minimum requirements are what are required but most government organizations actually do prepare the CHF area and within there we might provide more details to the smaller funds in part of the report and that'll give the reader of the report as much transparency as possible. They can see the major funds and then the ones that are interested in the allocation of the minor funds because Of course groups of people involved in those minor funds are gonna be interested can go into the details of the report and find the information that will be broken out for those more detailed smaller funds.

Governmental Operating Statement Accounts Government-Wide

In his chapter we will take a look at the governmental operating statement accounts government wide expenses and revenue. So we're concentrating here on the government wide activities as opposed to the fund statements to fund activities government wide classification reporting of expenses and revenues. Note that as we report this we're using the terms expenses and revenues an indication that the government wide activities as opposed to some of the fund activities are on an accrual basis as opposed to the modified accrual basis which will typically use expenditures in place of expenses.

We'll be discussing now the government wide statement of activities that's going to be similar to the income statement for a for profit type of organization. A government wide statement of activities displays net expenses or revenue for each function or program reported for governmental activities. And so the format then for each program or function will be the format of expenses first in the first column then we have the program revenues the difference being net expenses if it's bracketed or revenues if not this format can be a little bit confusing because he would expect Of course the revenues to be Bob for the expenses and we typically see it in a vertical fashion as opposed to a horizontal fashion. So let's take a look at an example. Here's a statement of activities for the City of Anaheim.

You'll note that we have the functions and programs we have for governmental activities including the general government, the police and the fire department business type of activities and then we have within the columns we've got the expenses, indirect expenses and then the program revenues. And that's going to give us basically the net over here to the right. So if we were to take a look at this then we're gonna say that and we'll take a look at examples of these which will make more sense later but just to get a format of this we're going to say that we have the one hundred seventy three seventy eight plus the three five four three minus the revenues which start with the charges for services which is going to be 1 5 3 6 1 minus the 6 7 9 3 minus the 9 9 7. That's what gives us our one fifty seven hundred and seventy here.

So you can see how that's going to be broken out by line item in terms of the functions and programs they are going to put the expenses first. Don't let that throw you off. And then we've got the program revenues broken out into these categories functions group related activities that are aimed at accomplishing a major service or regulatory responsibility like public safety programs group activities operations or organization or units that are directed to a specific purpose or objectives like highway betterment program revenues reported in the functions program chapters of the statement while the general revenues reported in a separate chapter at the bottom part of the statement.

So when we're thinking about the functions and programs then note we have those up top with the expenses and the revenue is going to be broken out up top. If we're talking about general type of revenue when we're considering general revenue that's not being broken out into the programs. We don't know where to assign it. There's no program or function to assign it to then those are gonna be included down here we've got the general revenues that are going to be added to the bottom. So breaking out the revenue expenses up top by line item by program and function.

And then when we have the general revenue which we're not applying to a particular program or function because as a general we have that down here including the taxes in this case property taxes sales and use taxes and so on and so forth program and general revenues program revenues are reported separately from general revenues and the government wide operating statements users can then evaluate whether functions or programs are self-sufficient or need general revenue to cover the costs. And that's going to be part of the reason that we have the breakout of the programs and the functions to see whether or not you know what type of funding that program or function has and needs program revenue categories charges for services charges to customers for both governmental and business type activities fines and forfeits license and permits.

We have operating grants and contributions restricted for operating purposes by other governments, organizations or individuals. And then we have capital grants and contributions restricted for capital acquisition by governments organizations or individuals. So you'll note that those are gonna be our categories up top when we have the functions and programs then we have the expenses and we have the program revenues broken out into our categories of charges for services operating grants and contributions and capital grants and contributions.

Items reported on separate line items below. General revenues in the statement of activity include special items within management's control and may be either unusual in nature or infrequent in occurrence. So those are going to be those items that possibly are in management's control but they're going to be unusual and infrequent and therefore we're breaking them out at the bottom of the income statement. Extraordinary items or events both unusual in nature and infrequent in occurrence.

So we have the and as opposed to the. Or this the differentiation factor, the key differentiation factor between these special items and extraordinary items. And then we have the Transfer transfer between the governmental activities and business type of activities.

Governmental Funds Characteristics

In this chapter we will take a look at governmental funds characteristics starting with the general fund. This is gonna be the most important fund. Every type of fund accounting is going to have a general fund with only one general fund. It's going to be the most important type of fund that we have other types of funds. We're going to apply as needed. We may have multiple other different types of funds but any type of governmental accounting any type of fund accounting will have a general fund and only one general fund. That's the first one we want to get a hold of.

Get a grasp of compare and contrast the general fund and the government wide type of activities general fund the primary governmental fund the accounting entity of a state or local government that accounts for current financial resources for the core governmental services. So note we're accounting for the current financial resources. The general fund like the. The governmental funds in general will be on the modified accrual basis. Then we have special revenue funds and we only set up special revenue funds when the circumstances require the setting up of special revenue funds. Unlike the general fund where we will always have one.

Also the special revenue funds may be situated so we might have multiple special revenue funds unlike the general fund which we will have one of special revenue funds generated when revenue sources are restricted by a donor or grantor or a tax or other revenue source is authorized by a legislative body for a special purpose. They show that all revenue from the restricted source was used for the special purpose. So for example we might have some type of revenue source some type of tax say we have a gasoline tax and we want to use the gasoline taxes just to fix basically the roads and we want to apply the revenue from the gasoline tax to fixing the roads well we might set up a special revenue fund then to make sure that the revenue from that specific source is then being applied as is given the requirement through legislation government funds include the general fund the major fund special revenue funds which we've just spoken of the debt service funds so we may have to set up debt service funds depending on the circumstances to help finance or track the long term debt such as bonds payable capital projects funds.

We may set up capital projects funds if we have capital projects where we want to track the revenue, the sources of revenue and the expenditures related to usually large projects. When you hear about capital projects you're thinking about something like building a building, building a library, building a fountain or something like a bridge or something like that. We want to basically track this information note. Then again we could have multiple capital projects at one time multiple CAD capital projects funds in order to attract those capital projects as opposed to the general fund where we have one.

We also might have no capital project fund as opposed to the general fund where we will always have one and only one then we have the permanent funds and that would be a situation only happening if we have a situation where we have a need for a permanent fund. What would that be like? What if someone gave money, donated money but they can only use the interest on the money or something like that. Or situations such as Weldon the principle of the fund of the funds are permanent they have to be held out forever and the interest would then be applied as was given the constraints of whatever the interest will be given for. Then we would have to set up a permanent fund in order to track the principal and then apply the or revenue as directed to the fund accounting equation. The fund accounting equation is in essence the same as the normal type of accounting equation that we thought of: assets equal Liabilities plus equity.

But remember that you can reformat the normal accounting equation from assets equal Liabilities plus equity to assets minus liabilities equals equity. That then emphasizes the balance of the equation. In other words it's emphasizing how much the assets are greater than the liabilities or the assets minus liabilities or the book value. In essence of the organization the value in terms of financial dollars of the organization the fund accounting is gonna be a little bit more complicated than that but those general categories are going to be the same general categories.

We're gonna have the current assets. Note that when we're talking when we're talking about governmental funds we typically are talking about current activity and therefore we have the current assets. Usually when we see a balance sheet for governmental funds we don't see any breakout of current versus long term because we're focusing in on the current activities the current flows then we have deferred outflow of resources which in essence you can kind of grouped together in current assets because of the modified accrual basis however we have something deferred outflow of resource it doesn't qualify exactly as the definition of current assets but these items will be increasing the net balance to fund balance and therefore at in terms of the accounting equation as similar to the assets would increase in the fund balance then we've got the current liabilities.

Once again we're talking about the current activities with the governmental funds. And so we typically won't see on the balance sheet for the governmental funds current liabilities versus the long term liabilities because we're focusing on the current type of activities. And once again because of the modified accrual basis we also have the deferred outflow of resources. These being islands that aren't defined exactly like liabilities therefore broken out differently in our category or definition. But in essence acting like liabilities there are going to be items that are going to decrease the fund balance.

What would be equivalent to like the equity chapter of assets minus liabilities that net assets type of act items. So we can think of it as basically the same type of accounting equation: assets equal Liabilities plus equity are assets equal liabilities now plus fund balance. So we're just changing the name of the fund balance. Then we're going to reformat the accounting equation to assets minus liabilities equal instead of equity fund balance. And then as we consider that accounting equation you want to break out that kind of nuance.

I would think of it as another nuance, another detail in that in the fund accounting equation we have something that it's kind of like an asset but isn't defined exactly like an asset and therefore is broken out into another category. So you could think of it as assets plus deferred outflow of resources minus liabilities current liabilities because we're talking about our governmental funds minus this thing that's like liabilities but doesn't isn't defined exactly as a liability and therefore we can think of it's broken out but acting as similar fashion as liability deferred outflow of resources and that then equals not the equity chapter as we would think of in a for profit organization but the equivalent to it in essence the fund balance. So note that this fund balance term assets minus liabilities equal in this chapter is something that's going to confuse people oftentimes because depending on what types of financials you're reading.

Obviously we have an equity chapter for a for profit organization. It could be referred to as fund balance. You can refer to it as net assets. So just note that you know whenever you see these types of terms you want to be able to have the specific term to the entity you're in but at the same time you also just want to recognize those terms as in essence functionally the same for the type of organization that we're talking about so functionally the equity chapter is much the same in terms of the fund balance as much as the same in terms of the net assets.

It just depends on whatever that type of organization we have and the convention that it's being used for that chapter. So here we have a statement of revenues expenditures and changes in fund balances for the City of Anaheim and you'll note that we have the revenues up top. Then we have the expenditures now we have expenditures rather than expenses because we're talking about the fund accounting which is on the modified accrual and this is one of the indications you have of that being the case you'll see not expenses but expenditures and you'll say are modified accrual type of basis where we're talking about the more current flow rather than the long term activity when we're thinking about the financial statements.

And then we've got the other financing sources and uses down below in this case including the transfers and transfers out and issuance of loan payable phoned operating statement accounts include revenues revenues being increases to fund financial resources other than from financing sources like inter fund transfers and debt issues other financing sources transfers to the fund and proceeds of debt issues and sales of general government assets. Then we have the expenditures which is kind of like the equivalent of expenses for accrual accounting modified accrual here cost to purchase of goods or services outflows of resources and then we have other financing uses transfers of resources from one fund to another. So in essence you have a similar kind of faction here, a similar factor where when we think about the income statement we would think revenue minus expenses.

Here we have revenue and then other financing sources, those items increasing what we would think of as net income or revenue over the expenditures. However, not being in the same category as revenue. So we're going to break them out but they act in a similar fashion. Of course we have the expenditures which are similar to the expenses for accrual accounting. This being the modified accrual accounting term for the similar actions. Similar item.

And then we have the other financing uses which act in a similar fashion as expenses decrease in what would be net income or do over expenditures but not exactly the same as expenditures. So again you can think of this as basically reading. These two items are revenues minus expenses. But I note a more nuanced view of it. We're going to say it's revenues minus the other financing sources which are going to increase the net income or the revenue over expenses and the same for expenditures versus the fire the other financing uses.

Budgetary Accounts

In this chapter we will discuss budgetary accounts because budgets are legally binding budgetary accounts have been integrated into the general ledger of the general fund. Special Revenue funds and other funds that are required by state law to use a budget from a for profit organization standpoint. This is very unusual because it means that we're actually going to be posting budgetary accounts to the general ledger in a for profit type of organization Of course we make budgets we think about budgets we project into the future we don't typically post the budget so this takes some getting used to once we understand it not too bad. But note that we're actually going to be posting the budgetary accounts because they're going to be legally binding.

If you're not used to this it'll be a little bit confusing at first it'll take some time to get used here and it will muddy the waters a bit when we consider the general ledger accounts especially those temporary accounts what would be the income statement type accounts because now we're going to have these budgetary accounts that are also posted to that area of what we would think the chart of accounts or the trial balance would be. Each operated account has a corresponding budgetary account. So when we're considering income statement accounts when we consider revenue and expenses or expenditures that revenue account typically has a credit balance it will usually have a corresponding budgetary account which will have the opposite or debit balance when we're considering expenses or expenditures.

Whatever the case may be it usually has a debit balance the corresponding budgetary account then having a credit balance. So the budgetary accounts have a normal balance that are the opposite of the corresponding normal account. So revenues have a normal balance of a credit. The budgetary revenue account will have a normal balance of a debit expenses or expenditures have a normal balance of a debit so the budgetary accounts for expenses and expenditures will have a normal balance of credit that typically being appropriations an account called appropriations as opposed to the revenue budgetary account which is called estimated revenue which is fairly self-explanatory appropriations doesn't have the word expenditures or expenses in it which is a little bit more confusing. We also have this encumbrances account as well that we will be dealing with and this technically is under the categories of budgetary accounts.

I would think of it a little bit differently when recording the information. And as we go through the actual posting I'll explain why this would be I would think of the encumbrances as kind of more of a holding type of account because the account that's going to be related to the expenses or expenditures that is going to be the budgetary account is going to be appropriations and then in conferences is gonna be kind of like the next step of assigning those appropriations out and it'll be kind of an interim step. So we're going to increase the in conferences and then decrease them before we can actually record or recognize the actual expenditure or expense on the accrual or modified accrual basis.

So I would think about the encumbrances as kind of a separate type of clearing account whereas the appropriations are gonna be basically the budgetary account. But when considering you know if you have to list a list of budgetary accounts you want to include the encumbrances in there just remember encumbrances are gonna be a little bit unusual a little bit different in terms of behavior and they're not going to follow this rule of having basically the opposite type of normal balance as the the main account meaning expenses or expenditures or the account that would be closely most closely related to encumbrances and conferences and expenses.

Both have normal debit balances because of the nature of both of them expenses expenditures and the encumbrances. This will become much more clear as we actually work through problems.

Fund Balance Sheet & Operating Statement Accounts

In this chapter we will take a look at and compare and contrast fund balance sheet and operating statement accounts as well as their complimentary budgetary accounts in a prior chapter. We took a look at the accounting equation and modified it for our fund balance sheet adding a few categories. In other words we have the accounting equation assets equal Liabilities plus equity.

We then converted to assets minus liabilities equals equity. That's going to be another way that we can see the accounting equation. And then we broke out within the fund account and we have the current assets because we're thinking about the short term flows. So when we think about balance sheet accounts the accounting equation type of accounts assets liabilities and equity or fund balance. In this case we're thinking about just basically the current assets and therefore not breaking out between the current and long term.

Given the fact that we're concentrating on the current flows and then we have this added category of deferred outflows of resources which aren't exactly assets but are going to be a result of a modified accrual basis and we'll increase the fund balance as assets woods so we can think of them in a similar category minus the current liabilities instead of current and long term we're basically saying current liabilities because we're looking at that short term cash flows once again. And then once again the deferred inflows of resources these being items that aren't the same as liabilities but have the same net effect on basically the fund balances we subtract them to get to the fund balance which would be equivalent to the equity chapter when we consider the categories we're talking about current assets which are going to be consisting of what we would expect for a fund balance sheet on the modified accrual basis cash receivables investments prepaid items inventories.

Notice these are all items that we would typically think of Of course as the current assets. That's what's going to be included in the fund balance sheet. We'll talk about more deferred outflows than being a consumption of net assets by the government that is applicable to a future reporting period. Then we have the current liabilities. Once again not current and long term consisting of what we would basically expect in current liabilities those being the accounts payable their crude liabilities noodles we don't have long term notes payable or long term bonds payable here in the fund accounting because once again it's that short term type of items the short term flows deferred inflows of resources and acquisition of Nest assets by the government that is applicable to a future reporting period.

Once again it will make more sense as we see transactions related to it. And that's going to be equivalent or equal to the fund balance which would be equivalent to the equity chapter of a for profit organization. You might hear other terms with regards to this item with regards to different types of organizations and you want to in essence be able to say oh that's part of the equity chapter for us. In other words assets minus liabilities could be named different things depending on the type of organization we've seen with business type of organizations it's usually called some type of equity either owners equity for a sole proprietorship partnerships equity or stockholders equity for a corporation and then we might hear something like net assets which is going to be the similar term for a type of organization we typically use the proper term here being fund balance for the for the fund financial statements but just realize when you hear those types of terms you should basically think the accounting equation think the balance sheet. So think of something like assets minus liability equals the net value of the organization with the fund balance here we have to realize that we need to break it out as well between those categories of non spendable restricted committed assigned and undesired and that's saying that hey look we have the assets minus the liabilities that's going to be the fund balance that's what people are going to want to start bidding over or tried to assign or try to get a piece of that value of that money.

And we have to say hey this is part of that fund balance that is either non spendable you can't we can't assign that out it's not spendable let's apply it out somewhere else in some way restricted committed assigned or unassigned and that gives some indication about the value the net value the assets minus what liabilities and what can be done with it operating statement accounts is it going to be equivalent to income type statement accounts for a for profit type organization include revenues and then we have other financing sources which are similar to revenues in that it'll increase what would be the net income or the revenue over the expenses or expenditures then we have expenditures and we also have other financing uses expenditures being similar to expenses for the modified accrual basis and other financing uses then being something that's going to decrease what would be net income for a for profit organization which would be revenue over expenses here but not being the same thing as an expenditure.

We'll take a look at these examples and these examples will become more apparent as we see transactions to record these items. Now we'll compare these to the counterparts within the budgetary accounts and remember that we actually post the budgetary accounts so when we consider if you think about the trial balance you're going to have these items on the bottom of the trial balance where the revenue and expense items would be under what would be the equity chapter or the net position type of accounts. And it's gonna be crowded down there because we have the revenue accounts.

What would typically be the normal kind of operating statement or income statement type of accounts. Revenue and Expenses now include revenue from other financing sources and expenditures which are like the expenses and replacing the expenses. And we're gonna have the budgetary accounts. The budgetary accounts included estimated revenues. So we are gonna have a revenue account and then a budget account of estimated revenues. Revenue has a credit balance. Estimated revenues than having a debit balance. And then we have estimated other financing sources. So we'll have other financing sources, the actual accounts and then it's gonna be a credit as well because it's similar to our revenue.

And then we have the estimated other financing sources which is gonna be our estimate of our budgetary account of what the estimated other financing sources will be. We're actually going to post that to the general ledger which will be on the trial balance now and it's going to be the opposite of the normal balance of revenue so it's gonna have a debit balance. Then we have expenditures which were our like expenses for the modified accrual basis. The related budgetary account not being the same in names that you have to just basically MEMORIZE IT IT'S GONNA BE appropriations. So appropriations are gonna be the budgetary account that's going to be similar to the expenditures. Expenses like expenses have debit balances. It's the expense type of account.

Therefore appropriations is gonna have the opposite of it because it's the budgetary related account which is going to be a credit then we have the other financing uses which acts kind of like expenses in terms of recording it and therefore the budgetary accounts are going to be estimated. Other financing uses other financing uses kind of like what the expenses would be. The expenditures having a normal debit balance bringing down what would be net income. Therefore the estimated other financing uses has a credit balance item for the budgetary account. And then we have this encumbrances and I put them into a category in and of themselves even though they're going to be under what would be the budgetary type of accounts I would separate it out in your mind as something like a clearing account and when we go through the problems I'll do that I'll I'll think about it separately and propose to think about it separately.

It's kind of a clearing account and what it's gonna do is going to be like an interim step with regards to the appropriations and when we can when we can record basically expenditures. So it's gonna go up and down in a bit different of rules than the budgetary accounts. I would think of the budgetary accounts as being something that we're going to record with one basic transaction. Have any adjustments we need to it and then reverse it all completely. The encumbrances are gonna be kind of a holding account that's going to increase and decrease in another kind of format that's a little bit distinct from what we would think of as the normal budgetary account. So be aware that if you're asked the question what are the budgetary accounts and you have to list them.

You want to include in conferences basically as the budgetary accounts they're there related to these items the appropriations related to kind of like the expenditure budgetary account but they're a little bit different and the same format and they don't follow the rule of expenditures having a debit balance. Therefore in conferences you would think you would have a credit if it's related. If it's the budgetary equivalent it does have a debit and this will become more apparent when we go through it. So I would think of it this way in your mind. If you have a test question: Is it a budgetary account? Yes. If you're thinking about how we record these things these are going to be the budgetary accounts that line up specifically to the income statement or the operating statement accounts and then the encumbrances are kind of its own.

It's in its own world I would think of and we'll explain what that world is and how it's used much more clearly as we think through examples. With regards to actually posting the budgetary accounts and more importantly in this hit with the encumbrance account the specific budgetary account which is more kind of like a clearing account a little bit different little bit distinct note that if we post these items to the general ledger we actually post the budget we're going to end up in essence with estimated revenues and estimated expenditures or appropriations and that's going to result in an estimated net something a net revenue or expense so we're going to put that somewhere where we're going to put that.

Well we don't know where to put it. So we're going to include an equity type of account. That's typically what happens when we do something kind of funny and we need to include a holding account somewhere within basically the equity chapter on the balance sheet side of things. Now within the fund balance or what would be at the equivalent of the equity chapter for a for profit organization we're going to include the budgetary account which is just going to be called budgetary fund balance. So the budgetary fund balance is going to balance out the equation we're going to post this items estimated revenues the equivalent of you know like estimated revenues estimated other financing sources the appropriations and the estimated other financing uses and the difference the balance of it then is going to go to the equity chapter and the budgetary fund balance.

And if there's any adjustments we'll make adjustments to it. But those financial journal entries will always basically reconcile at the end of the time period when we close things out. We will in essence reverse that transaction by taking it off the books. Exactly and it'll all work out nicely and again that'll make more sense once we do the examples. So what our appropriations specifically legal authorizations to expend cash or other financial resources for goods services or facilities needed for specific reasons amounts cannot exceed amounts authorized for each reason. So when we think about the appropriations note we're going to have people that want to assign this money out.

Normally with accrual accounting what we end up doing is saying when we have the expense we're going to record the expense on an accrual basis when we have actually consumed the expense than we recorded here. We want to say has it been legally authorized already for spending in the future because our goal is to be as transparent as possible so we don't want to wait to the point in time that the expense would be recorded under an accrual basis.

We want to actually make it very transparent to people say hey we already have the appropriations. These have been assigned out. These are the specific appropriations and therefore we put the budgetary account on there and we want to systematically be able to show what the appropriations are and whether they have been used or not appropriation is expended when amounts authorized and appropriation have been incurred.

So when we think about the expense related account which is expenditures what we're basically saying hey look we have the appropriations what we assign this money to be we've already assigned it there and now we're gonna say that it has been incurred at this point in time record in the not the expense but the expenditure on the modified accrual bases and therefore the term expenditures instead of expenses is called is what the expended appropriations and expenditure then is the expended appropriation.

Revenue Sources & Classifications

In this chapter we will take a look at revenue sources and classification. Revenue generally includes all financial resource inflows. Revenues are classified by fund and then by source and then by secondary class source classes of revenue include taxes special assessments license and permits intergovernmental revenues. Charges for services and fines and forfeitures. Tax revenue recognized on a modified accrual basis so modified accrual as opposed to the cruel the accrual basis recognized when revenue is measurable and available when we think of the accounting bases we typically think of a cash basis versus and accrual basis and somewhere in between are usually going to be some other type of basis such as a modified accrual basis.

We can generally think of it as kind of a hybrid between a pure tax base or pure cash base or a pure accrual base. Whenever we think about a method also we're typically thinking of when we recognize revenue. When do we recognize expenses? So when do we recognize revenue in our cash bases? When do we recognize revenue under an accrual basis and then under the modifications any kind of modified method typically being somewhere in the middle in terms of when we would recognize revenue and expenses here being under the modified accrual on the revenue side recognized revenue.

When measurable and available tax types include property taxes, sales taxes, income tax and death tax or estate tax as well as interest and penalties can be included Of course in the taxes. So these are going to be the taxes that can be assessed to government agencies then having the right Of course to tax that's going to be one of the major revenue sources available if the taxes aren't paid then they have the ability to assess interest and penalties on them which we can consider in essence part of that taxation. Tax recognition.

Revenue from sales tax and income tax is recognized in the period at which the underlying event takes place. So when we're talking about taxation related to sales tax and income tax we're going to apply them to the related item in terms of the sales tax. When did the sale happen? That's the period that we want to apply the sales tax to in terms of the income tax. When was the income earned and that can get a little bit messy Of course because when was the income earned. When did the sale happen? Could be a different date than when the sales tax is actually paid or even assessed.

In other words Of course we have to know how much income we earned and then know what our tax rate is in order to calculate what the appropriate income tax would be. So we have in essence a timing difference where , from a cash basis, we're not recognizing these items or the revenue related to the sales tax and income tax when we receive them. We're going to recognize them when basically the triggering event happened which is closer to what we would think of as an accrual basis under an accrual basis. We recognize revenue when we have earned it. Here we're saying Well when have we earned it we're recognizing it basically at the triggering event and that's going to be the point of sale and the income earned as opposed to waiting until we receive that revenue in order to record it.

Intergovernmental revenues grants and other financial assistance are transactions in which one government transfers cash or other items of value to or incurs a liability for another government an individual or an organization as a means of sharing program costs subsidizing other governments or entities or otherwise reallocating resources to the recipients that per Gatsby license and permits. Another form of revenue would be licenses and permits could include building permits, vehicle licenses, business licenses and animal licenses or different types of licenses.

We could have, which Of course would result in revenue. Governmental revenue of some kind. Charges for services. What kind of services could a government charge? We have court costs. We have parking meters. We have recording fees. We have special police service. Tuition and zoning fees are all areas where we have charges for services provided more of a kind of a business type of activity that you expect from governments in other words service being provided revenue being generated charges for the service or in alignment with the goods and services being charged.

Encumbrances & Expenditures

In this chapter we will talk through and walk through the process of recording and conferences and expenditures. This being one of the more confusing items because it involves budgetary account appropriations which doesn't sound like any of the two accounts that we typically think of. And like a normal type of income statement account revenue and expenses but is related to the expense type of accounts with the budgetary account that would be related to the expense type account except that we don't typically have just expenses the expenses are now called expenditures and then on top of that we have the budgetary account which doesn't really act like a normal budgetary account more like a clearing account as will explain when we go through examples of conferences.

Therefore this is usually one of the more confusing processes and it's one that we'll spend a lot of time with with examples that make a lot more sense. Once we go through these with examples and actually post these out post the budgetary account for appropriations post and conferences and then the related expenditures so we'll go through it in words here then we'll go through a lot of examples about that about this and that's when it really get more concrete revenue sources and classifications. At this point in time we're going to say that we have already posted the budgetary accounts of appropriations. Then the next thing that's going to happen is a purchase order or some kind of contract, some type of estimate of the purchase order and contracts are reviewed to see if a valid appropriation is there. So in other words we're gonna say hey there's an appropriation on the books we set up the appropriation which is in essence an estimate of what we think the expenditures will be.

We've recorded the appropriations. Then when we have a purchase order and you can consider and think of the purchase order similar to what we would have in terms of a purchase order for a for profit organization the purchase order is kind of that strange type of document that we're going to record we're going to send it to the vendor in a for profit organization but we don't record a journal entry related to it. In other words if we wanted something like inventory we wanted to order the inventory we'll fill out a purchase order we'll send it out to the vendor hoping that they're gonna give us the inventory.

But at the time of the purchase order we have not paid for the inventory, we have not received the inventory and therefore there is no financial transaction on our books yet we're not going to record anything, we're going to track the fact that we sent out a purchase order. We're going to hope and expect that we're going to receive inventory for that purchase order but we won't record the inventory or the payment for it or the billing of it until we receive the inventory or until some type of payment happens. And in this item we're gonna say that once we issue the purchase order we're actually going to record this item because what we're saying is we want to be very transparent here in terms of what's going on not just recording a financial transaction but where the funds have been assigned to. So we're gonna say we actually record the budget which means that the appropriation is on the books now meaning we've already assigned in essence where we think this money is gonna go. Then we review the purchase order to see if it's valid in accordance with lining up with the appropriation.

And at that point in time we do kind of a funny thing which is we actually record that we're going to say we're going to record that the appropriation is encumbered for the amount of the purchase order or contract. So now we have the appropriation on the book books and we still haven't got the inventory we haven't paid for it. We just sent out the purchase order but we're actually going to record what we're going to record like the purchase order which is again something we don't typically do and for profit accounting and the purchase order is going to increase the encumbrance account. And the other side's gonna have to go to an equity type of account and I would call this more of a clearing type of account.

All this is saying hey is like here's the budget and now we've even more committed to it by actually approving a purchase order which is basically what we can think of as an estimate of the incompetence has now been approved. And basically the purchase orders out or the contract is there although we have not yet paid for it and therefore can't record what would be kind of like the expense under a normal type of accrual system or cash system but we want to record the fact that we've committed to the purchase order or contract and therefore we're going to record this encumbrance. And then when goods of services are received and the invoice is approved, record the appropriations being expended. So then what we're gonna do is we're basically going to reverse the encumbrance that we recorded which is just basically recording the purchase order. It's just like a holding account.

And then once we actually have the expense that we would think of as a more normal time period when we would record it when a financial tracked transaction actually happens with regards to what would be related to IT expense expenditures. Well that actually takes place then we record what we would think normal transactions would be increasing the expenditure and crediting a payable or cash at that time. So the process is going to be looking like this: we're going to record the appropriation. That's the budgetary account. So we're gonna say Hey we're gonna record the appropriation and put it on the books. We've. That's us estimating in essence what the expenditures the income statement account related to expenses will be.

We've already basically estimated it and assigned them then we're gonna have the encumbrance. That's when we're really committed to the item with a purchase order or an estimate or a contract that we've approved and assigned out the appropriations to that contract. We're gonna record this and what I would call a clearing account which is kind of but it's still like a budgetary account but I would call it a clearing account a holding account an interim account because we cannot yet record the actual expense under an accrual basis or modified accrual basis yet because we haven't received anything and we haven't paid for anything. So there's no financial transaction under a normal accrual process.

Nothing triggers the actual financial transaction but we want to be transparent that the appropriation has now been committed to a specific contract or purchase order. And then we're gonna have the actual expenditure when we have the expenditure. That's when the normal triggering process would happen under what would be similar to an accrual basis or cash basis when a financial transaction has happened. We can recognize the expenditure on the modified accrual basis in accordance with the modified accrual basis rules as we do so then we're gonna have to reverse the encumbrance because the conference is gonna be on the books just as a holding account until we actually record the expenditures.

So you can't have these two in the books relating to the same item. This encumbrance is a holding account until we're able to record the expenditure at that point of time. We have to reverse and remove the encumbrance that is related to the expenditures that have now been incurred and recorded.

www.ingramcontent.com/pod-product-compliance
Lightning Source LLC
Chambersburg PA
CBHW062351290526
45794CB00005B/2180